The Star-Spangled Banner

Illustrator: Peter Spier

Publisher: Doubleday, 1973 (Available in Canada, UK: Doubleday; AUS, Transworld Pub.)

Summary: This is primarily a beautiful picture book designed to match the words of the national anthem. Historical information of the time period is also included in the text.

Related Holidays: Labor Day, Veterans Day, 4th of July

Related Songs: "America," "You're a Grand Old Flag," and "The Stars and Stripes Forever," Wee Sing America (Price/Stern/Sloan, 1987)

U. S. Flag—1777

Related Bibliography

Crews, Donald. *Parade.* Morrow, 1986.

Graham-Barber, Lynda. *Doodle Dandy! The Complete Book of Independence Day Words.* Macmillan, 1992.

Haskins, Jim. *Count Your Way Through Canada.* Carolrhoda Books, 1987.

Scott, Geoffrey. *Labor Day.* Wyman, 1982.

Williams, Susan. *Canada.* Bookwright Press, 1991.

Connecting Activities for Labor Day

- Ask your students to share their future job and/or career plans in small groups upon completion of the activity titled "Your Job!"
- Make a chart of the types of jobs held by the parents of students in your classroom.
- Invite parents to speak to the class about the careers they have chosen. Prepare for each speaker by learning something about the job before the parent comes in to speak. Be ready to interview the parents after they talk about their jobs.
- Learn about labor laws in the United States. Have students write letters to the government requesting information. (They may want to specify interest in child labor laws.)
- Have a local labor union representative speak to your class. Allow time for a question-answer session. Have students write thank you notes.
- Tell students to look closely at pictures of the men on the big ships in The Star-Spangled Banner. Then talk about some of the jobs or duties they might have had to perform in order to maintain the ships.
- Discuss the ways in which new technologies are changing some of the jobs of the past in our country.
- Ask students to draw pictures depicting their family celebrations of Labor Day. Then divide the class into small groups and have students share their art work.

The Star-Spangled Banner (cont.)

Connecting Activities for Independence Day

- Create a mural of a parade. First, show students the wordless book by Donald Crews entitled *Parade.* Discuss with the children who and what might be in a 4th of July parade. Then prepare a strip of blue butcher paper as a background. Add details such as brown paper for the ground and roads, green grass, trees, or whatever else the class wants to add. Make construction paper characters to place in the scene. Finally, title and hang in an appropriate place.

- Organize a bicycle parade. Have the children decorate their bikes with streamers, balloons, pictures, flags - anything red, white, and blue. Encourage them to add lots of detail to the bicycles. If a bike parade is not possible in your area, have a patriotic pedestrian parade. The children can wear red, white, and blue hats, carry flags, and perhaps even play some small drums and cymbals.
- Plan a special theme day around clowns since they are a fun part of many parades. Let the children put on some simple washable makeup to look like clowns and have them decorate construction paper cones for hats. If possible, arrange for a clown to visit the class and show how he or she puts on makeup. Talk about how clowns design their own makeup so that they have a unique look. Show pictures of some famous clowns such as Emmett Kelly, Red Skelton, and Ronald McDonald.
- Ask everyone to look closely at the pages of *The Star-Spangled Banner* and note that flags can be seen in many of the pictures. Then discuss with the class various locations where flags might be seen today. Finally, have students write paragraphs describing what the U.S. flag means to them. Upon completion, they may share their work with partners.
- Extend your study of this holiday by comparing it to Canada's celebration of Dominion Day. Talk about the origin and purpose of the holiday and the similar ways in which it is celebrated. There are several excellent books available to assist you in gathering facts about Canada, including *Canada* by Susan Williams and *Count Your Way Through Canada* by Jim Haskins. The former contains a wide variety of information on Canada's climate, products, holidays, transportation, and much more. The latter describes many aspects of Canada by counting from one to ten in French.

The Star-Spangled Banner (cont.)

Connecting Activities for Veterans Day

- Have several students take turns reading or singing the lyrics found in *The Star-Spangled Banner* aloud while others act out the words using props.
- Tell children to observe the picture in *The Star-Spangled Banner* on the double page that says "Oh, thus be it ever when freemen shall stand." Talk about the reason for flying a flag at half mast. Have students research other ways a flag may be used to signal something.
- Plan a time for students to witness and/or participate in the raising and lowering of the flag at your school.
- Invite a veteran to come and speak to the class about his/her experiences.
- Talk about the military that exists today. Discuss the fact that now both women and men may serve our country. Brainstorm ideas regarding the differences between war and peacetime duties.
- Ask students to draw pictures showing what they think military uniforms of the future might look like.
- Have children create a classroom display using the military cut-outs found in this book.
- Divide the class into small groups and have them discuss the meaning of the word "peace."
- Sing patriotic songs together. Include those with titles mentioned at the beginning of this literature unit.

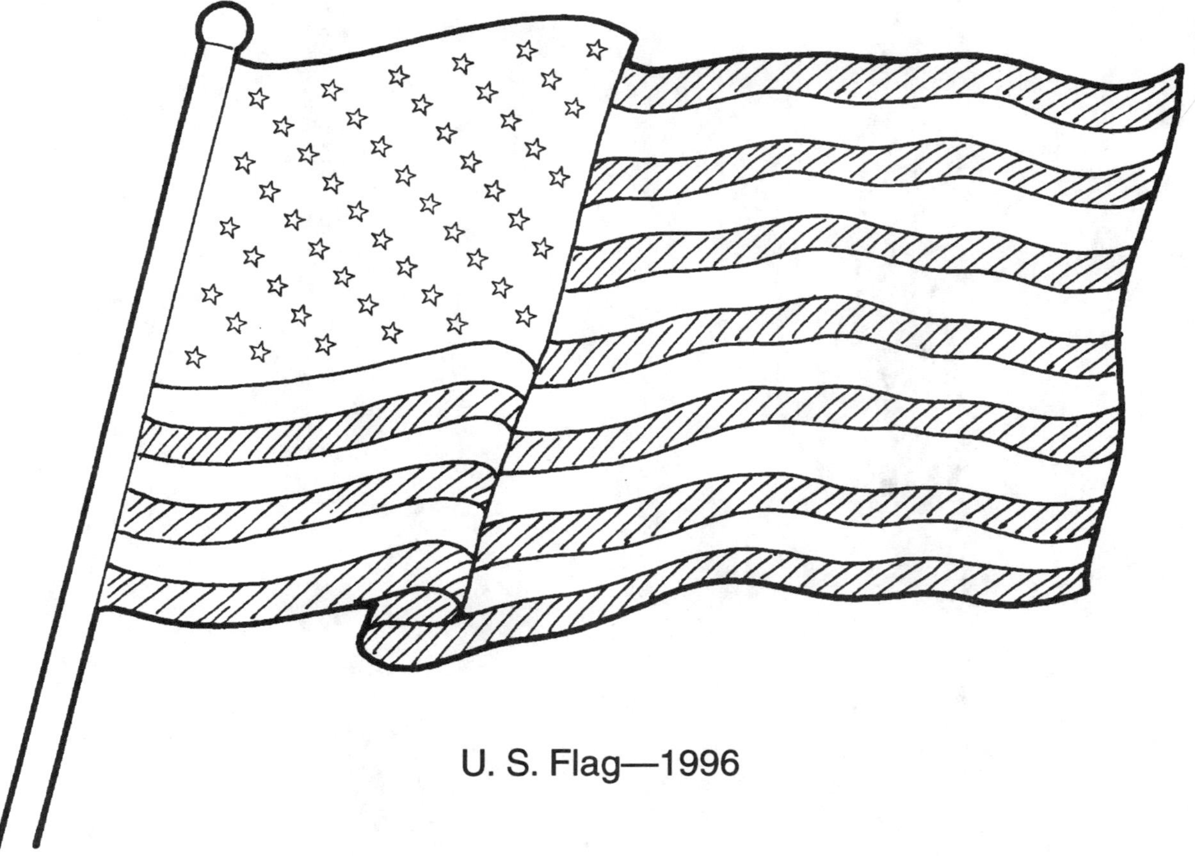

U. S. Flag—1996

Labor Day

To labor means to work. Labor Day is a national holiday that honors all people who work by giving them a day off to rest and "play." It is celebrated on the first Monday of September. But there was not always a Labor Day. The idea for a Labor Day began over 100 years ago in New York City.

The people in New York City and other places throughout the country wanted to work. They took pride in what they did. But the conditions they worked under were not the best. They often worked long hours, sometimes 12 to 14 hours a day, six or seven days a week. Laborers were underpaid and worked in places that were not safe. By the time children were 11 or 12, they often had to work to help support the family, and their workday was usually 10 hours.

The unhappy workers joined together to form unions, which united people in the same trades. These unions were able to speak in a louder voice to make their needs known. Some of the smaller unions joined together to form a Central Labor Union. These union members fought to get better working conditions. Along with improved conditions for work, they also wanted a special holiday to honor all laborers.

The first Labor Day was organized by the New York Central Union and scheduled to be on Monday, September 5, 1882. It was a huge success. Over 10,000 workers marched in the parade and over 50,000 people filled Elm Park for a day of picnics, speeches, music, and family fun. The day ended with fireworks.

Workers throughout America liked this idea of Labor Day. The next year, hundreds of cities held Labor Day celebrations. And in 1894, Labor Day became a national holiday.

We continue to celebrate Labor Day in the tradition of those workers of long ago. We have a day off work and school, sharing food and fun with our families and friends.

"You've Got A Raise"

A Labor Day Card Game

Players: Two or three

Directions:

1. For each set of cards, reproduce 3 copies of the career card page that follows.
2. Cut out all cards. Throw away two copies of the card that reads "You've Got A Raise!" There will be 33 cards to a set.
3. Mix the cards, face down. Deal 5 to each player. Put the remaining cards in a pile face down.
4. If a player is dealt four identical cards, he or she makes a "book" of these and places them face up in front.
5. After the players have eliminated their "books" from their playing hands, the first player selects an unseen card from the pile. Then the player checks to see if he or she can make a "book" with this additional card.
6. The second player then takes a turn.
7. The player who ends up with the "You've Got A Raise!" card wins.

Variations:

- Two identical cards can also make a "book." This enables the game to be played at a quicker pace.
- This game can also be played like "Go Fish" or "Old Maid."

"You've Got a Raise" (cont.)

Career Cards

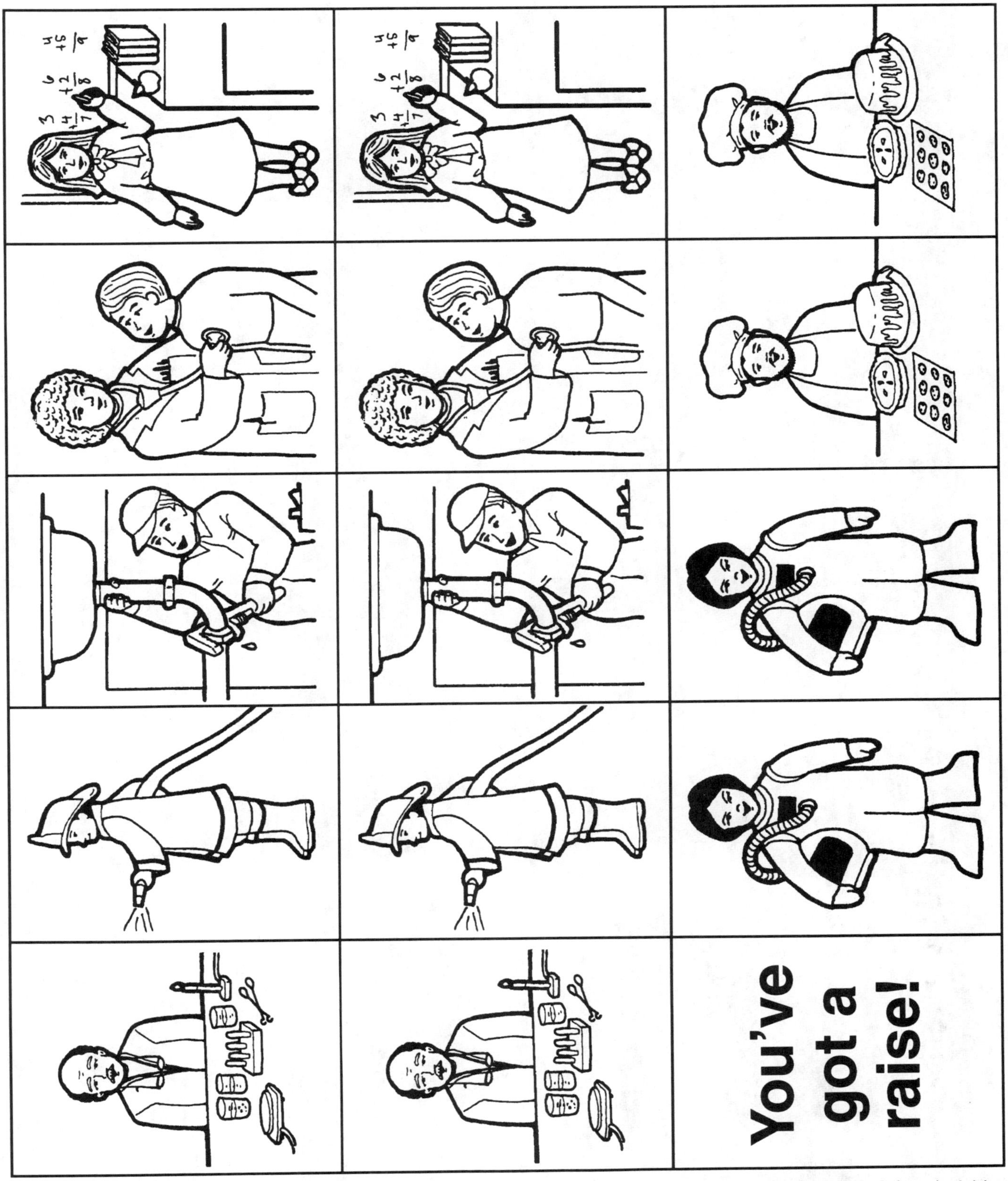

You've got a raise!

Your Job!

What kind of job would you like to have in the future? What type of training will you need to have for this job? Do you think you will be able to get this kind of job? Is it the kind of job that will make you happy? Complete this job description form.

My Job!

My name: ____________________

The job I want to have in the future: ____________________

____

Job Description: ____________________

____

Schooling or training I will need to have: ____________________

____

Approximate salary: ____________________

____

Why I think I would be good at this job: ____________________

____

Good points about this job: ____________________

____

Points that are not so good about this job: ____________________

____

Someone I know who has a job like this: ____________________

____

Veterans Day

Veterans Day is a day that honors those men and women who have served their country in the United States Armed Forces. November 11 is the day these special people are honored.

In our country, Veterans Day was not always known by that name. On November 11, 1918 (the 11th hour of the 11th day of the 11th month), World War I ended. This was known as "The War to End All Wars" and people the world over rejoiced. The day became known as "Armistice Day" in honor of the truce of peace that was made on this day.

Armistice Day became a day to recognize those people who had fought so courageously in World War I and to celebrate the peace that now existed. November 11 was designated as a federal holiday in 1938. But shortly after this holiday was declared, World War II broke out. The dream of "The War to End All Wars" was now gone. Many lives were lost during this second world war, and those who lost loved ones and those who fought for their country needed to be recognized as well as those World War I patriots.

In 1954, Congress changed the name of Armistice Day to Veterans Day, in order to honor all United States veterans. At this time, President Eisenhower asked all Americans to strive for peace.

In the United States, people remember Veterans Day with celebrations, parades, speeches, and special services. It is a day to honor all the veterans who have served our country.

United States Marine Corps War Memorial

Military Uniform Cut-Outs

Here are a male and female figure you can use to display the uniforms on the following pages. You may also wish to check with recruiting offices of the various branches of the military service for models of uniforms. Color and cut the figures. Color keys are provided.

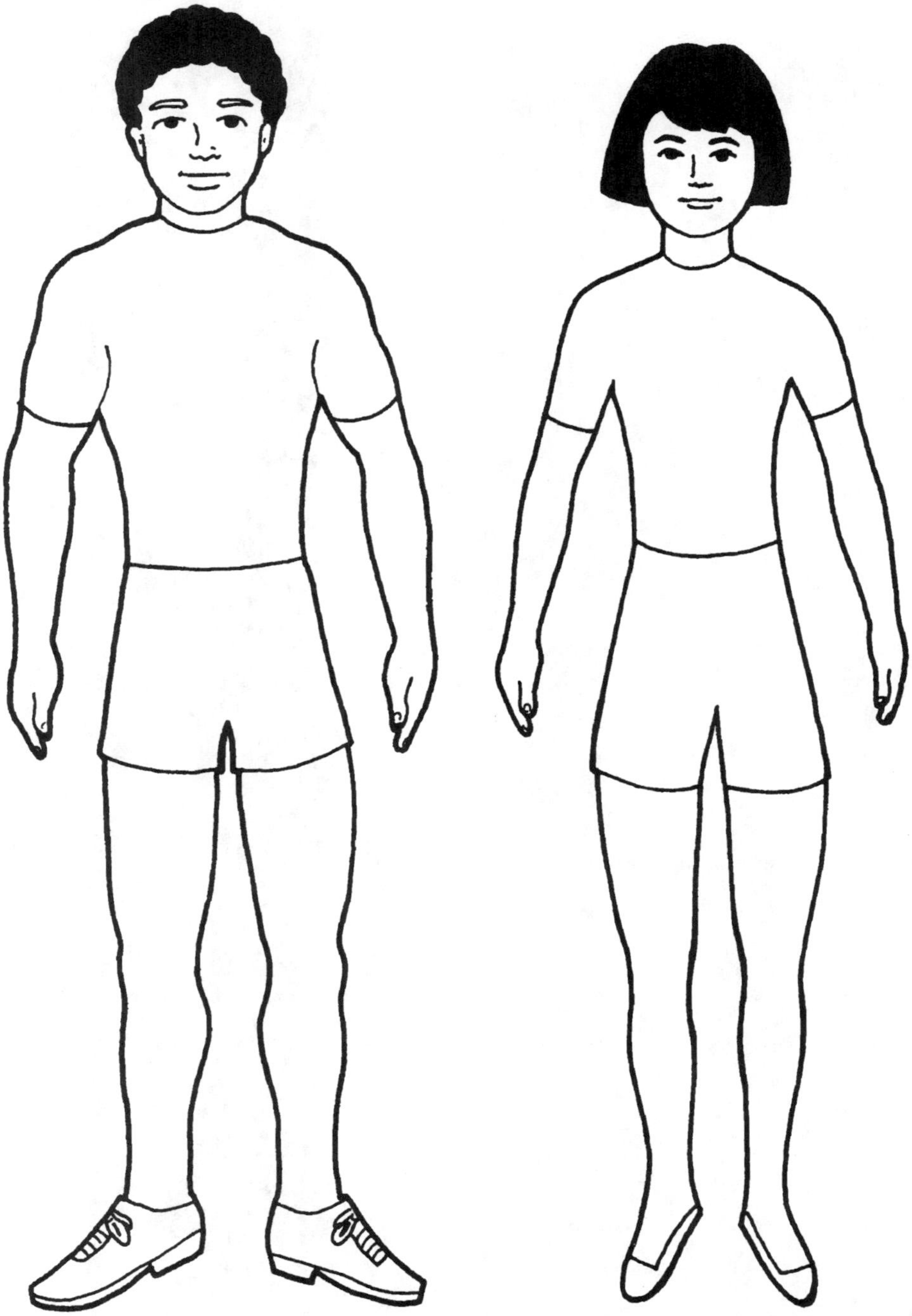

Color Key:

t-shirt: *white*

shoes: *black*

Army

The U.S. army is the branch of military that is trained to fight on land. The Army also helps during natural disasters, builds public works, and improves harbors and inland water ways. Dating from June 14, 1775, the Army is the nation's oldest branch of the military.

Color and cut out these Army uniforms. Use them on the figures found on the previous page.

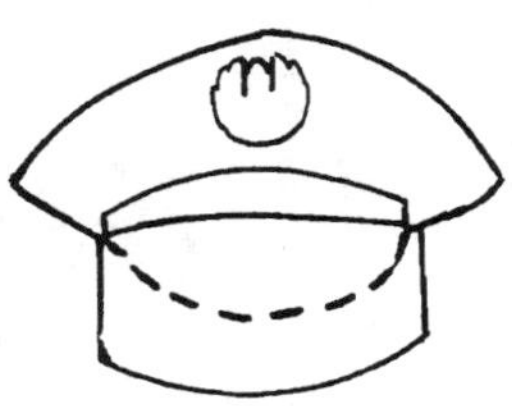

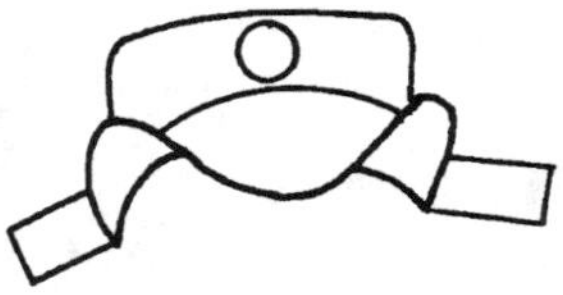

Color Key:

pants: *green*
jacket: *green with gold buttons*
insignia: *gold and black*
tie: *black*
shirt: *white*
shoes: *black*
hat: *green with gold insignia and black flap*

Navy

Commanding the seas is the job of the U.S. Navy. During peacetime the Navy is involved in helping to maintain international relations. The navy had its beginning during the Revolutionary War.

Color and cut out these Navy uniforms. Use them on the figures found earlier in this activity.

Color Key:

pants: *navy blue*

skirt: *navy blue*

jacket: *navy blue with gold buttons and gold stripes*

shirt: *white (men); navy blue with red stripes and white badge (women)*

shoes: *black*

hat: *white with navy blue trim*

Marines

The branch of the U.S. military that deals with amphibious assault operations is the Marine Corps. Marines are always at the ready. In 1775 the Continental Congress established a marine corps.

Color and cut out these Marine uniforms. Use them on the figures found earlier in this activity.

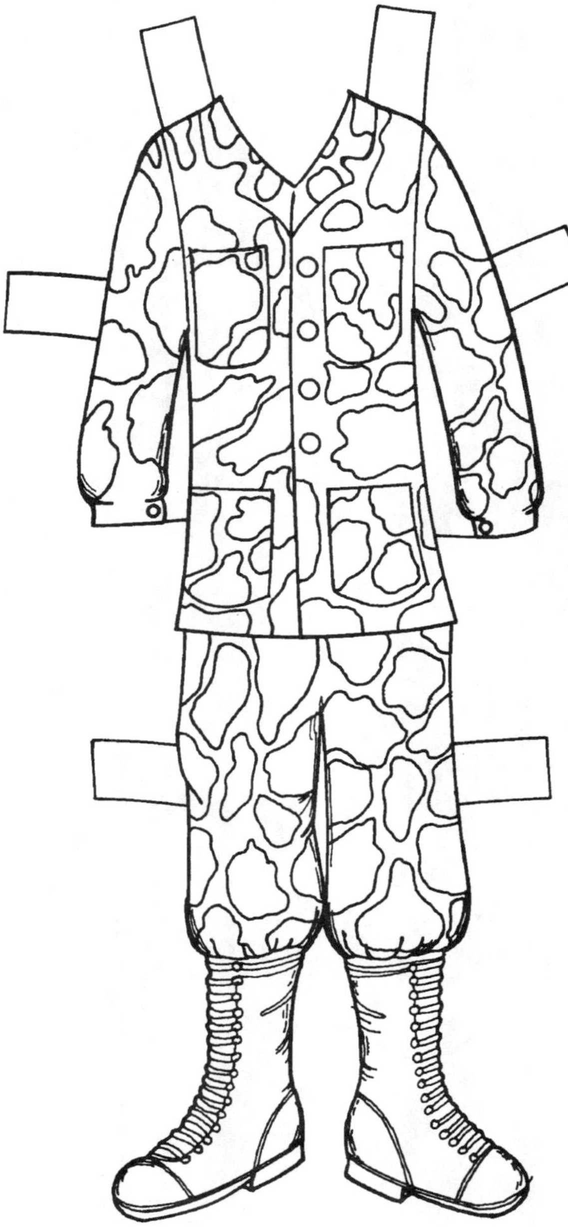

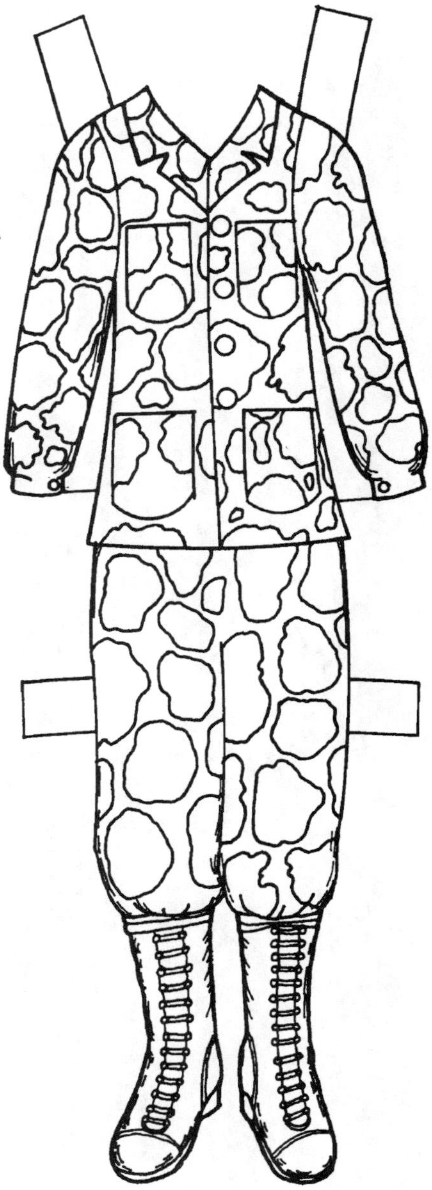

Color Key:

pants: *camouflage*

jacket: *camouflage*

helmet: *camouflage*

boots: *black*

Air Force

Military responsibility for air and space falls to the United States Air Force. The Air Force was officially established by Congress in 1926.

Color and cut out these Air Force uniforms. Use them on the figures found earlier in this activity.

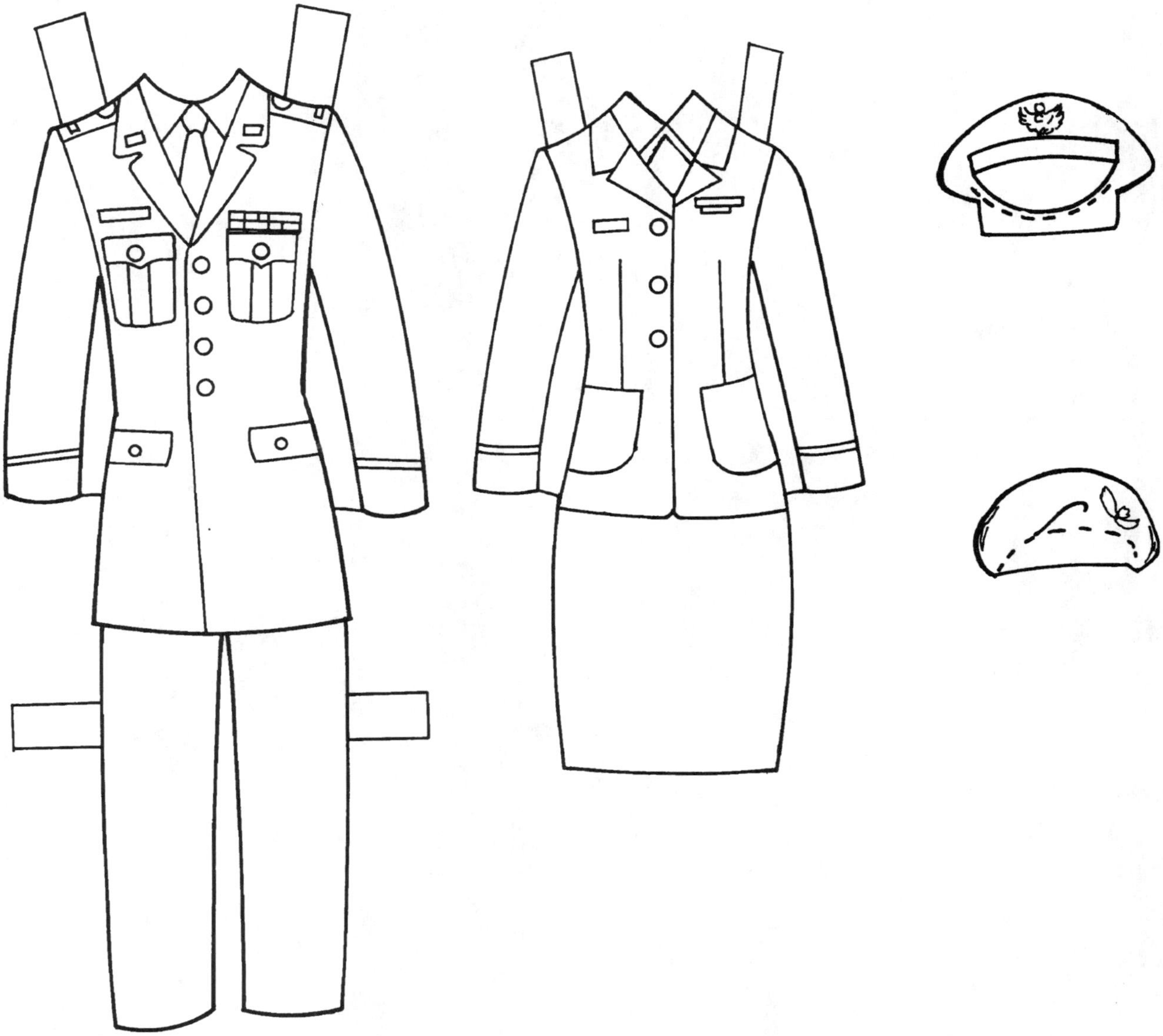

Color Key:

pants: *navy blue*

skirt: *navy blue*

jacket: *navy blue; silver insignia, buttons, and badges*

shirt: *white*

tie: *navy blue*

shoes: *black*

Independence Day

On Independence Day, the Fourth of July, the people of the United States celebrate the anniversary of the founding of our democratic nation. The signs of the holiday are everywhere. Flags are unfurled around the countryside, people cover the parks and recreation areas with picnics, Uncle Sam leads town parades, patriotic music fills the air, and spectacular fireworks light up the sky! It is a noisy, joyous day!

Independence Day is the birthday of the United States. On July 4, 1776, over 200 years ago, the United Colonies of America adopted the document which declared the United States to be "Free and Independent States," and that "all political connection between them and the State of Great Britain, is and ought to be totally dissolved." This document was the Declaration of Independence which gave all who lived in these new United States the equal right to "Life, Liberty, and the Pursuit of Happiness."

The Declaration of Independence set up the foundation for freedom and democracy in our country and inspired many people throughout the world to be free.

The first Independence Day celebration took place in Philadelphia on July 4, 1777. It was a grand day of festivity. Through the years, the Fourth of July has been kept as a special holiday by the people of the United States. It's a day filled with historic remembering, a rededication to democracy, and a whole lot of fun!

Honoring Our Flag

The flag of the United States is a symbol to be treated with respect. Here are some rules for displaying the flag with honor. Cut out each of these boxes that hold the rules. Paste or glue them under the appropriate pictures.

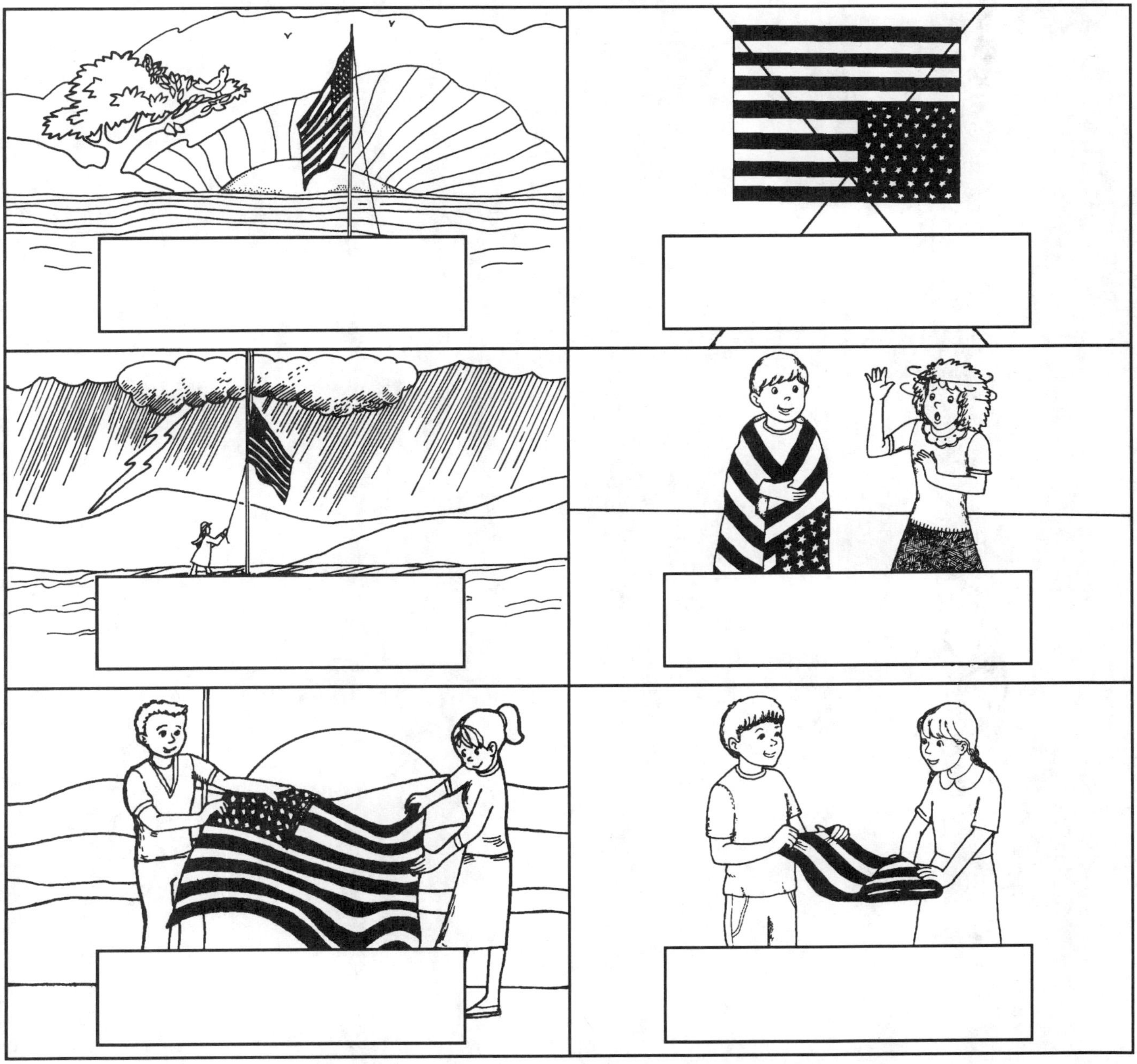

Do not display the flag if the weather could damage it.	Do not hang the flag upside down. That signals a serious emergency.	Carefully fold the flag when it is not being displayed.
Do not let the flag touch the ground.	The flag of the United States may not be used for clothing. Use the colors, not the flag.	Display the flag from sunrise to sunset.

4th of July Bike

Directions: Pretend that you are going to ride this bike in a 4th of July parade. Design and color it the way you would like it to look.